Andrew Lloyd Webber
Vocal Duets

ISBN 978-1-4234-2745-2

HAL•LEONARD® CORPORATION
7777 W. BLUEMOUND RD. P.O. BOX 13819 MILWAUKEE, WI 53213

For all works contained herein:
Unauthorized copying, arranging, adapting, recording or public performance is an infringement of copyright.
Infringers are liable under the law.

Andrew Lloyd Webber™ is a trademark owned by Andrew Lloyd Webber.

The musical works contained in this edition may not be publicly performed in a dramatic form or context
except under license from The Really Useful Group Limited, 22 Tower Street, London WC2H 9TW

In Australia Contact:
Hal Leonard Australia Pty. Ltd
4 Lentara Court
Cheltenham, Victoria, 3192 Australia

Email: **ausadmin@halleonard.com.au**

Visit Hal Leonard Online at
www.halleonard.com

CONTENTS

ASPECTS OF LOVE
- 3   The First Man You Remember
- 10   Seeing Is Believing
- 16   She'd Be Far Better Off with You

THE BEAUTIFUL GAME
- 22   All the Love I Have
- 26   Don't Like You
- 34   The First Time
- 42   To Have and to Hold

CATS
- 46   Gus: The Theatre Cat
- 53   Memory

THE PHANTOM OF THE OPERA
- 60   All I Ask of You
- 74   The Phantom of the Opera
- 65   The Point of No Return

REQUIEM
- 82   Pie Jesu

STARLIGHT EXPRESS
- 86   Only You

SUNSET BOULEVARD
- 92   Too Much in Love to Care

THE WOMAN IN WHITE
- 106   I Believe My Heart

OLYMPIC THEME
- 100   Amigos Para Siempre (Friends for Life)

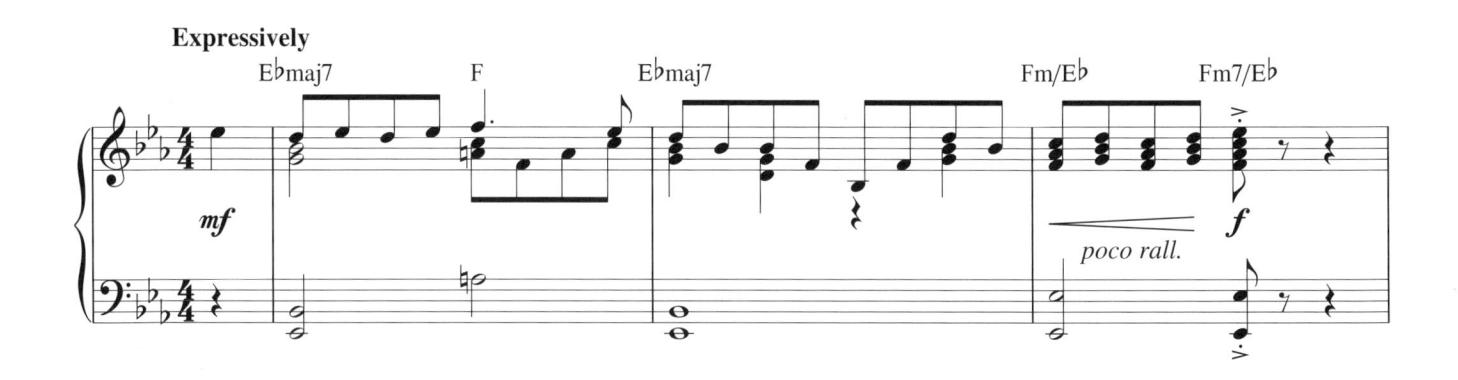

The First Man You Remember
from *Aspects of Love*

Music by Andrew Lloyd Webber
Lyrics by Don Black and Charles Hart

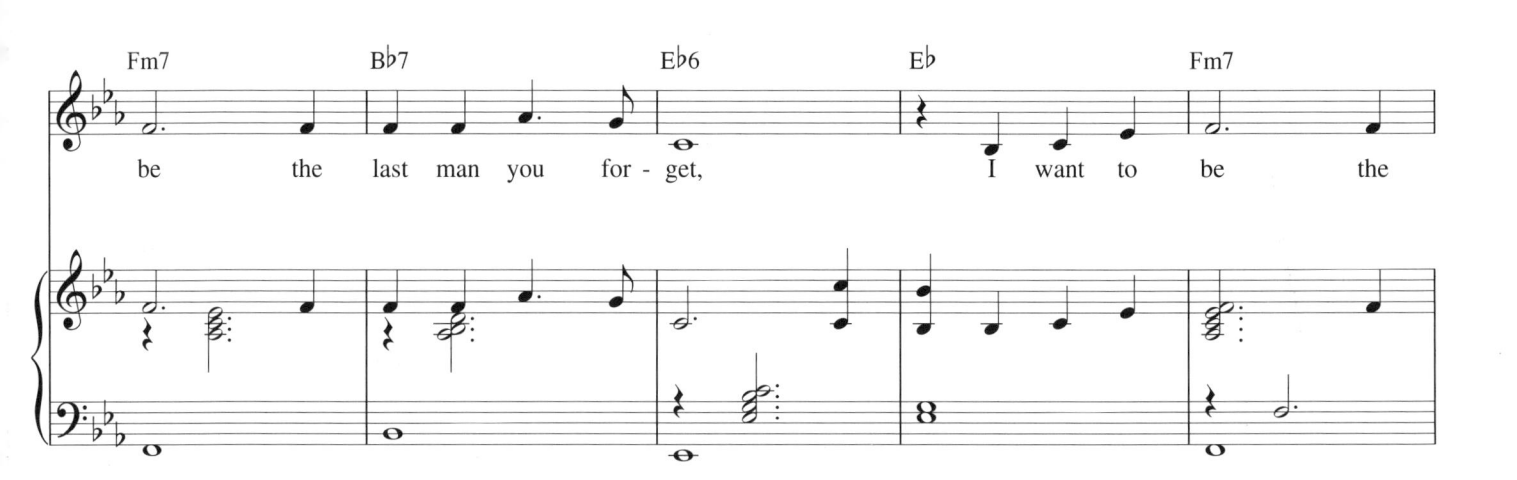

GEORGE:
I want to be the first man you re-mem-ber, I want to be the last man you for-get, I want to be the

one you al-ways turn to. I want to be the one you won't re-gret. May I be first to say you look de-light-ful? May I be first to dance you 'round the floor? The ver-y first to see your face by moon-light, _the ve-ry first to walk you to your door?_

poco più mosso

JENNY: Well, young man, I'd be de-light-ed! There is noth-ing I would rath-er do! What could be a sweet-er mem-'ry than shar-ing my first dance with you? I want to be the first man you re-mem-ber. The ver-y first to sweep me off my feet. I want to be the one you al-ways turn to. The first to make my young heart miss a

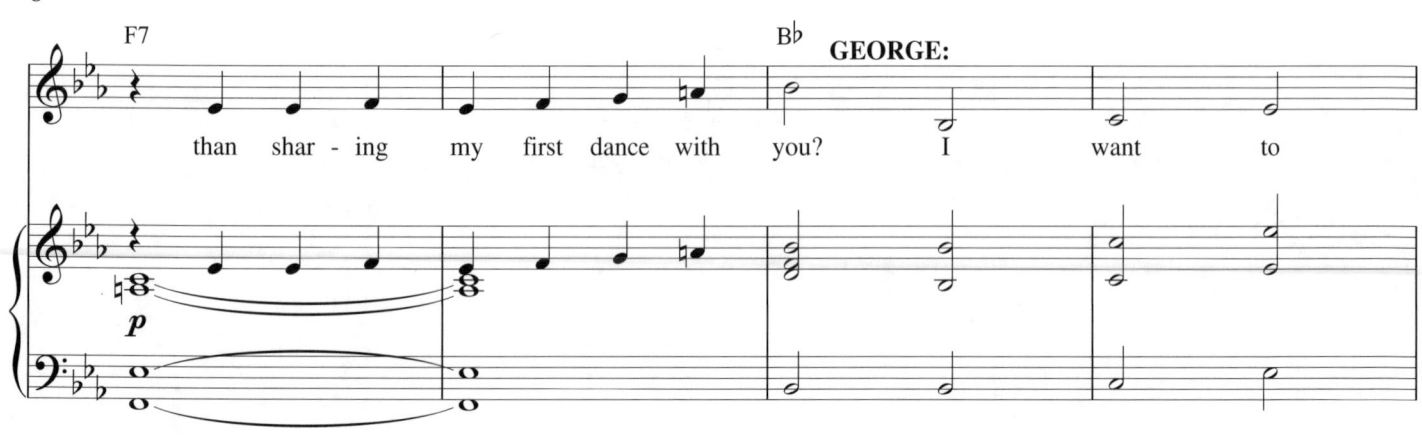

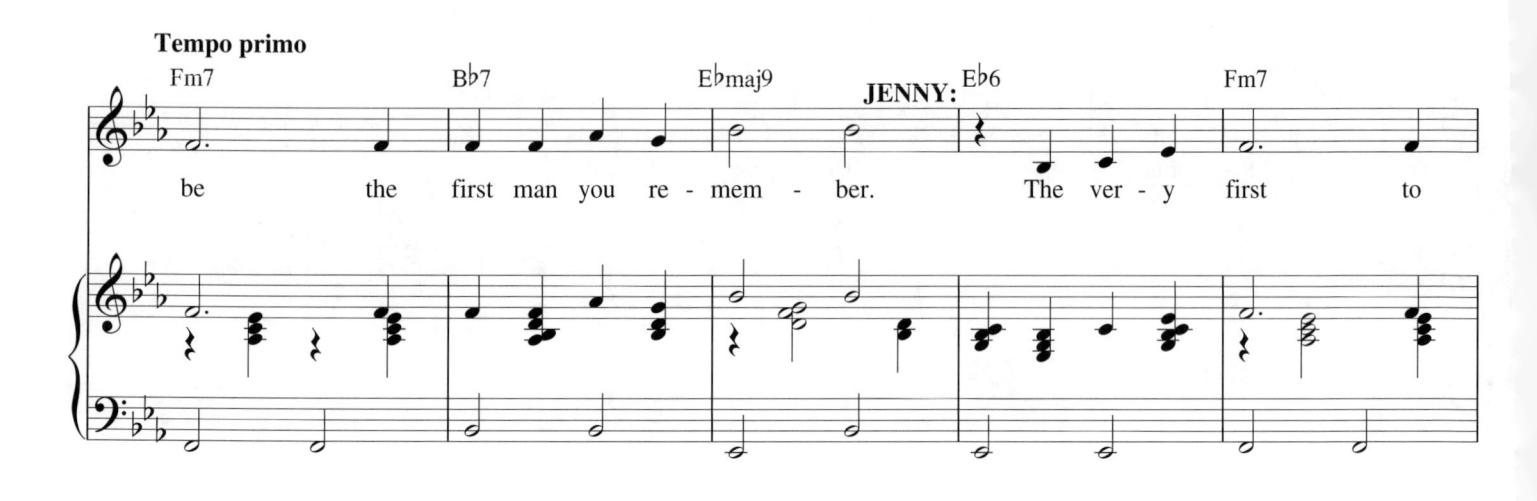

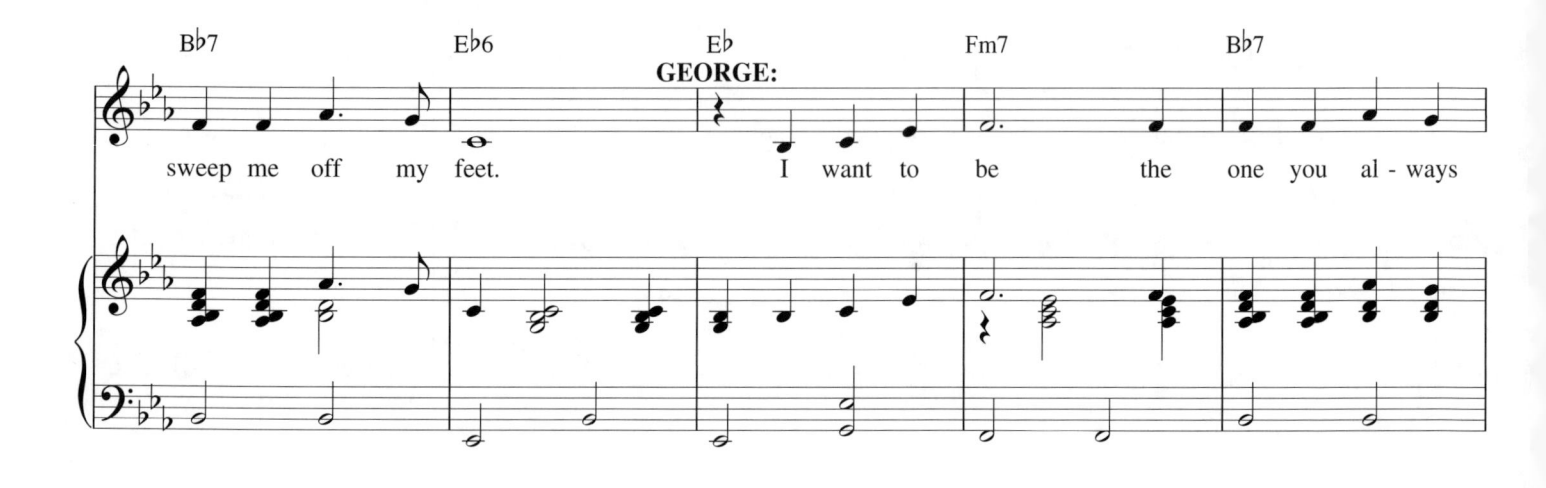

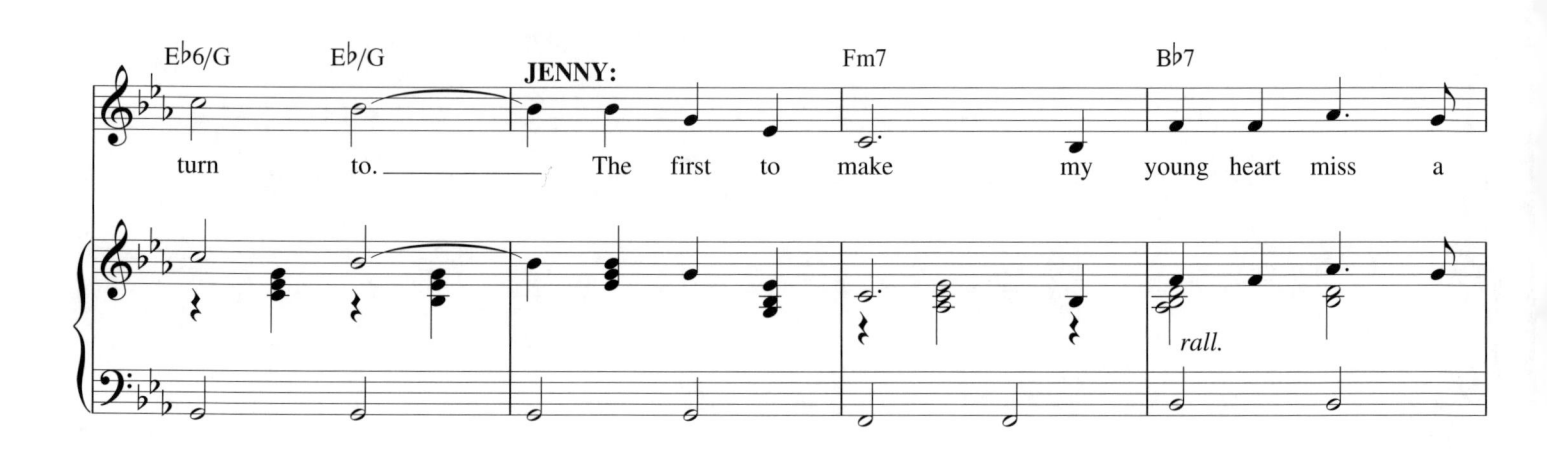

Opt. cut to **

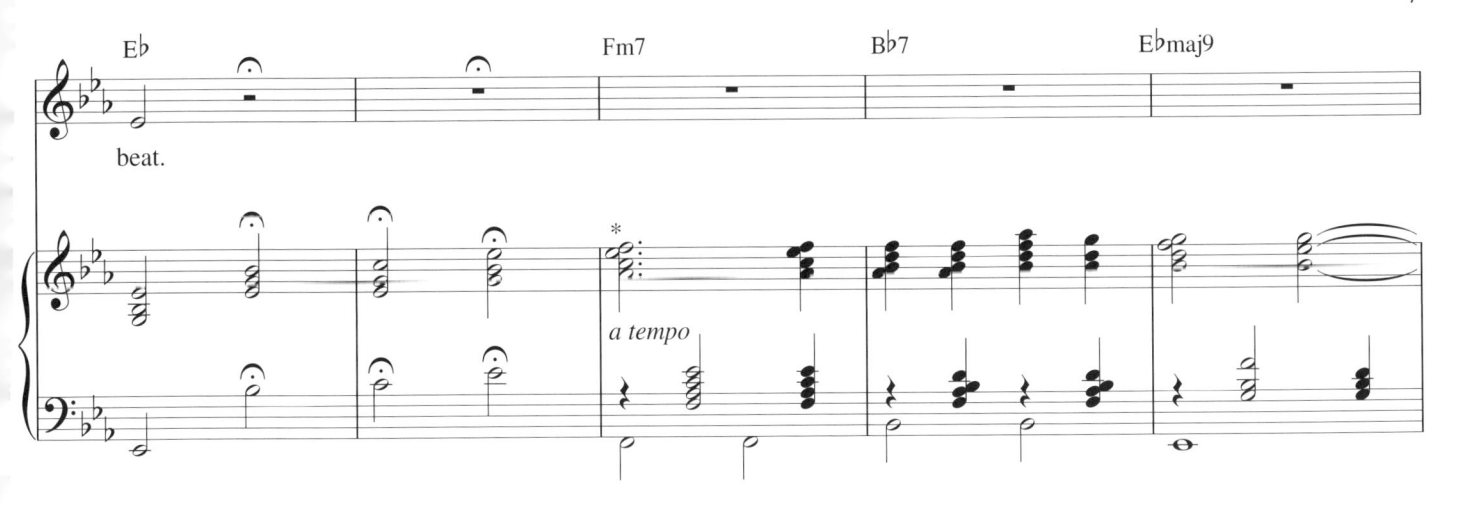

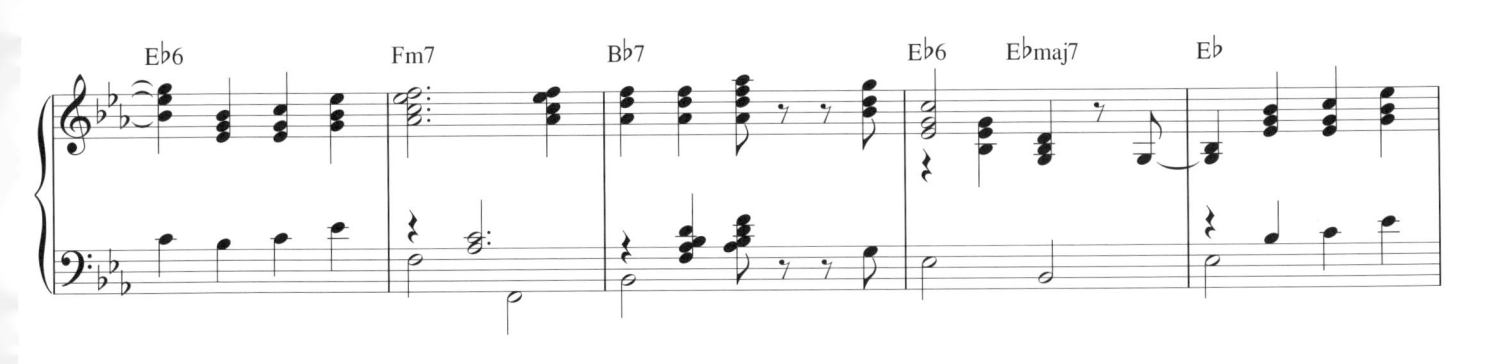

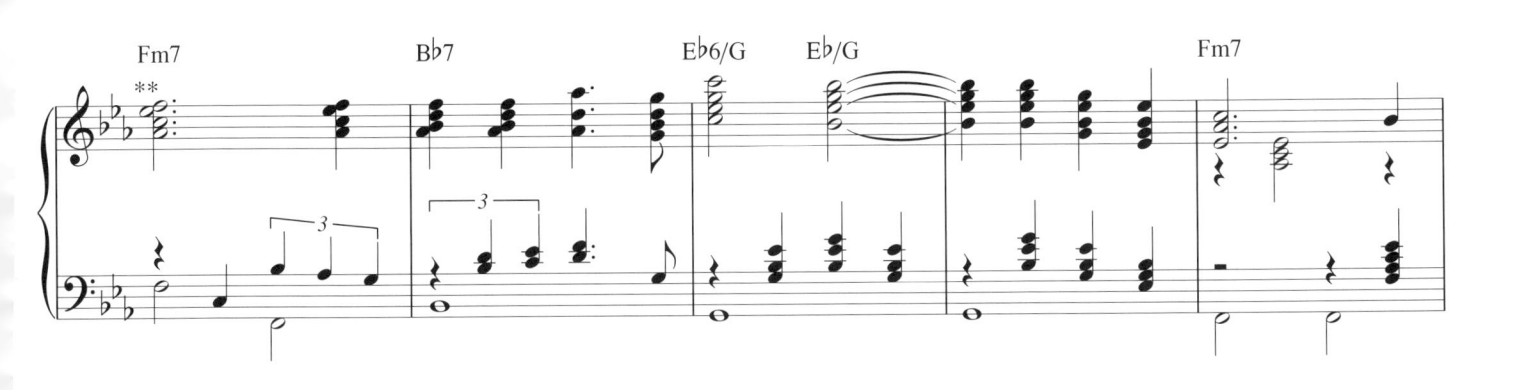

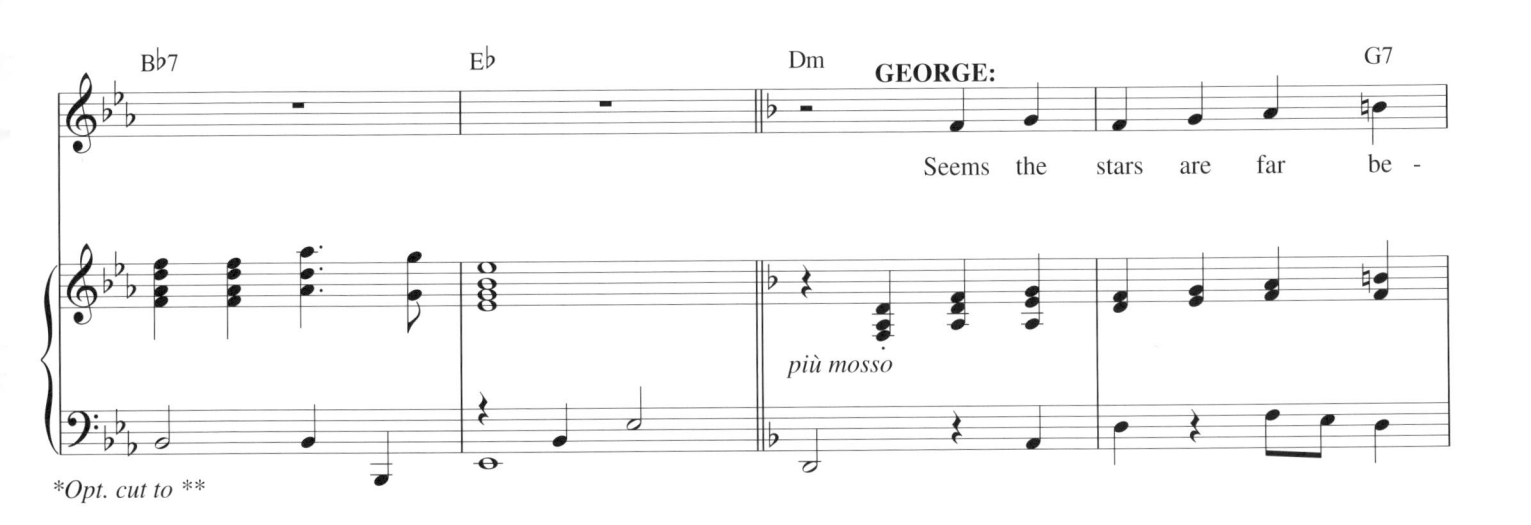

GEORGE: Seems the stars are far be-

C
Dm
JENNY:
A7
Dm
low us.
The moon has nev - er felt so close be -
Am
C7
Gm7/C
C7
fore!
Our first dance will
F6/C
F/C
Dm
G7
GEORGE:
be for - ev - er.
And may it lead to man - y
poco rall.
còmodo
Meno mosso
C
F♯
F♯6
G♯m7
C♯7
F♯(add2)
F♯
more.
rit.

G♯m7
C♯7
F♯6
GEORGE:
G♯m7
C♯7
F♯6/A♯
I want to be the one you al - ways turn to.
poco rit.
F♯/A♯
G♯m7
C♯7
F♯
I want to be the one you won't re - gret.
G♯m/F♯
F♯
G♯m/F♯
F♯
JENNY:
The ver - y first.
BOTH:
The ver - y first.
rit.

Seeing Is Believing
from *Aspects of Love*

Music by Andrew Lloyd Webber
Lyrics by Don Black and Charles Hart

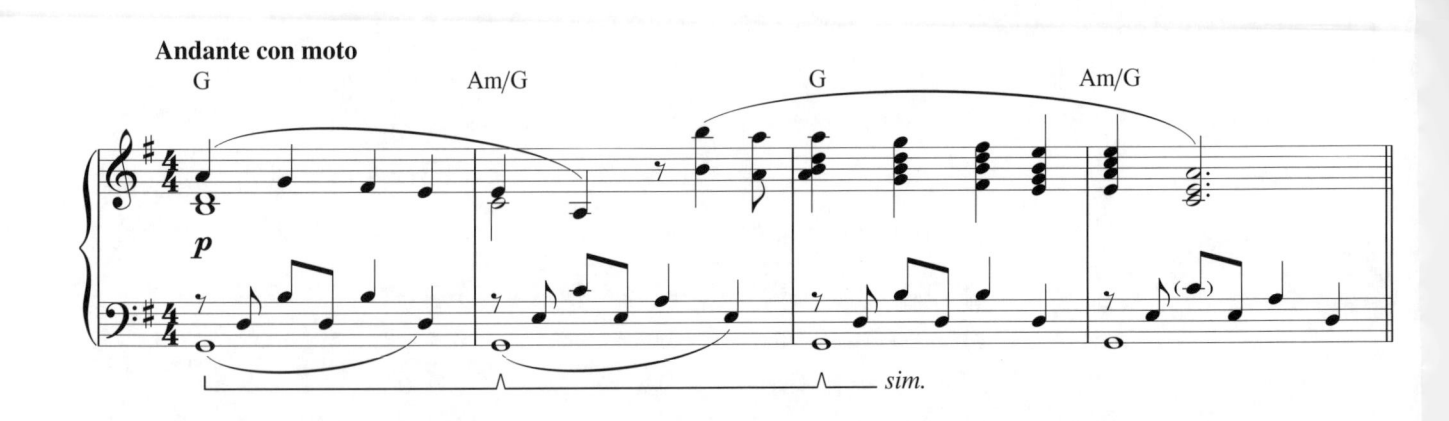

Andante con moto

ALEX:
See - ing is be - liev - ing, and in my arms I see her: she's here, real - ly here, real - ly mine now.
See - ing is be - liev - ing, I dreamt that it would be her: at last life is here, full, life is fine now.

© Copyright 1989 Andrew Lloyd Webber licensed to The Really Useful Group Ltd.
International Copyright Secured   All Rights Reserved

1
Am7
Bm
2
Am
Em
She seems at home here...
What-ev - er hap-pens, one thing is cer-tain:
poco meno
poco più mosso
Am
Bm/A
ten.
Am
each time I see a train go by, I'll think of us, the
ten.
Bm
A7
C/D
D7
G
Am/G
night, the sky for - ev - er.
rit.
a tempo
sim.
G
Am/G
G
Em
Bm

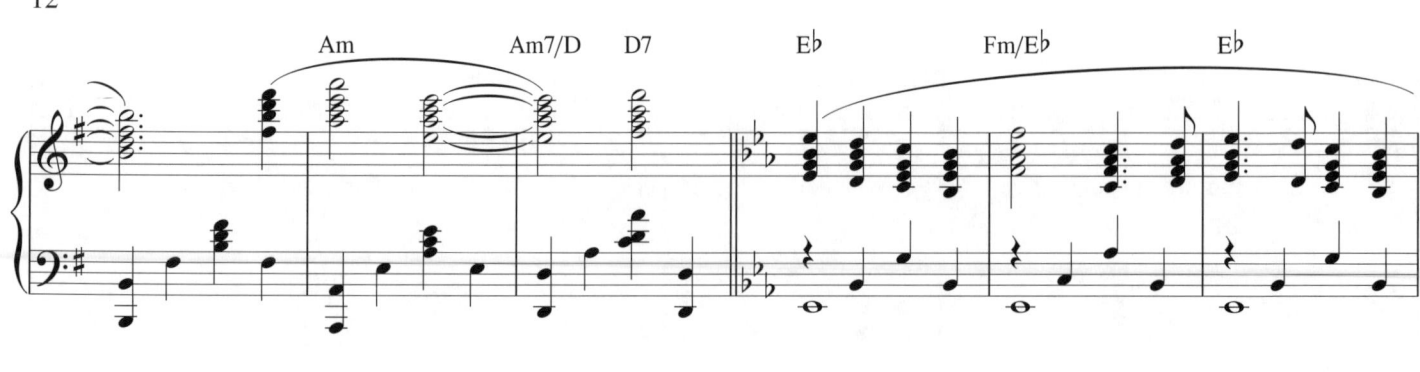

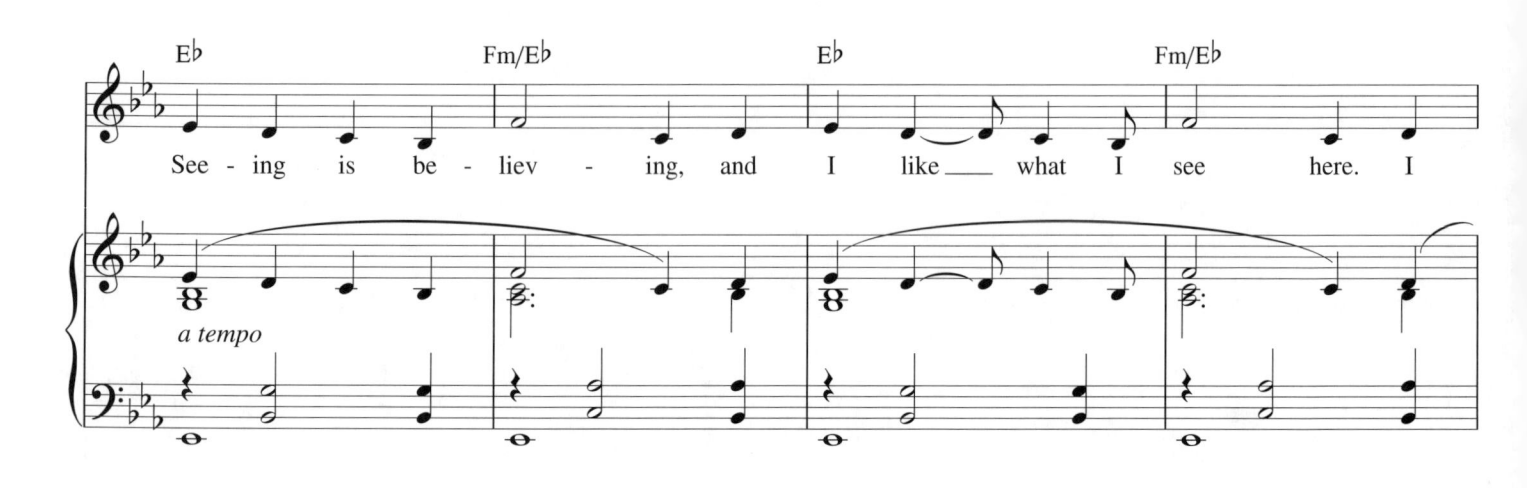

ROSE: He's young, ver-y young, but ap-peal-ing. I feel I know him...
(MALE) Alternative: She's warm and she's wild and ap-peal-ing. I feel I know her...

See-ing is be-liev-ing, and I like what I see here. I like where I am, what I'm feel-ing. What are we do-ing?

13

never thought I'd be here. Is this really me, am I dreaming? No way of knowing where this is leading, it's fun forgetting who we are. Who cares when now the world is far behind us.

Tempo primo
G♭ A♭m/G♭ G♭ A♭m/G♭
See - ing is be - liev - ing! My life is just be - gin - ning! We
ff
sim.
G♭ E♭m B♭m A♭m7
touched, and my head won't stop spin - ning from win - ning
allarg. e. cresc.
A♭m7/D♭ D♭7 G♭ A♭m/G♭ D♭7/G♭ G♭
your love!
a tempo
p cresc. molto
f

She'd Be Far Better Off with You

from *Aspects of Love*

Music by Andrew Lloyd Webber
Lyrics by Don Black and Charles Hart

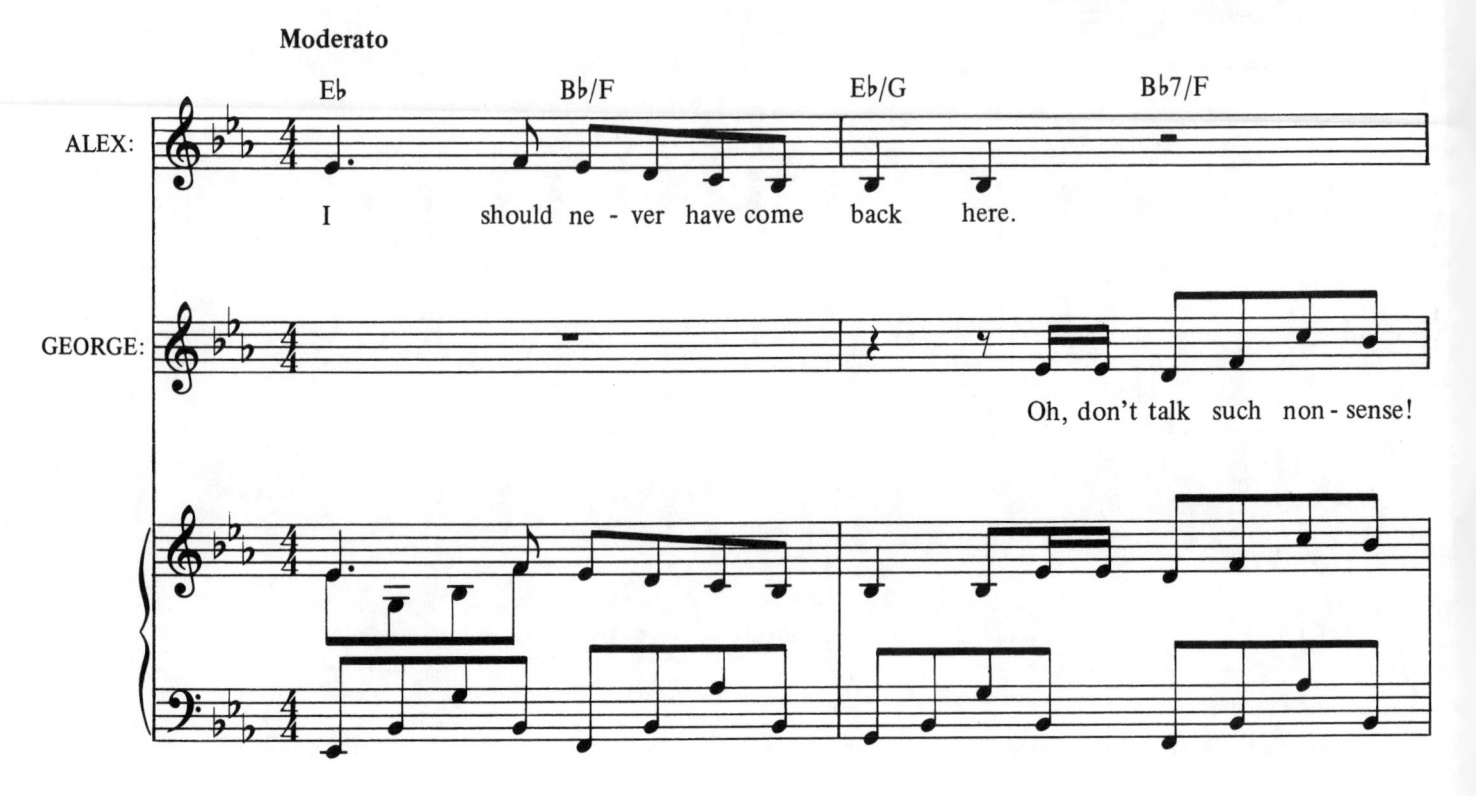

Moderato

ALEX: I should never have come back here.

GEORGE: Oh, don't talk such non-sense!

ALEX: I'll bow out now, it's the decent thing to do.

GEORGE: Don't be ab-

© Copyright 1989 Andrew Lloyd Webber licensed to The Really Useful Group Ltd.
International Copyright Secured   All Rights Reserved

I'm a dis-as-ter. It would-n't last a week. She'd be far bet-ter off with
-surd. Oh come, come.

you. It would end in mur-der.
You two have your lives be-fore you. I'm too old for her. It's

Your place is here. It's the
high time I with-drew. The jowls are drop-ping.

light.

The paunch needs prop-ping up. She'd be far bet-ter off with

Your words are gen-er-ous and self-less but a-las un-true.
you. Your words are gen-er-ous and self-less but a-las un-true.

She'd be far bet-ter off with... You are steeped in wit and
She'd be far bet-ter off with you.

19

wis - dom. You could teach George Ber - nard
Well I've learnt the odd thing.

Shaw a thing or two! You've dined with Gar - bo, trans - la - ted "La Bo - hème"
I had a go. On - ly twice.

She'd be far bet - ter off with you. You're dis -
You're ath - le - tic.

-tin - guished. You're more sea - soned.
You don't cheat at cro - quet. You can

You're in "Who's Who." We're talk-ing dri-vel. Can't we be ci-vi-lised?
skate. Just half an inch. So we are. Can't we be ci-vi-lised?

She'd be far bet-ter off with you. Your words are gen-er-ous and self-less but a-
She'd be far bet-ter off with you. Your words are gen-er-ous and self-less but a-

- las un-true. It's on-ly Rose that mat-ters! Just take a look, there's no com-pa-ri-son be-tween us two. She'd be far bet-ter off with you.

All the Love I Have
from *The Beautiful Game*

Music by Andrew Lloyd Webber
Lyrics by Ben Elton

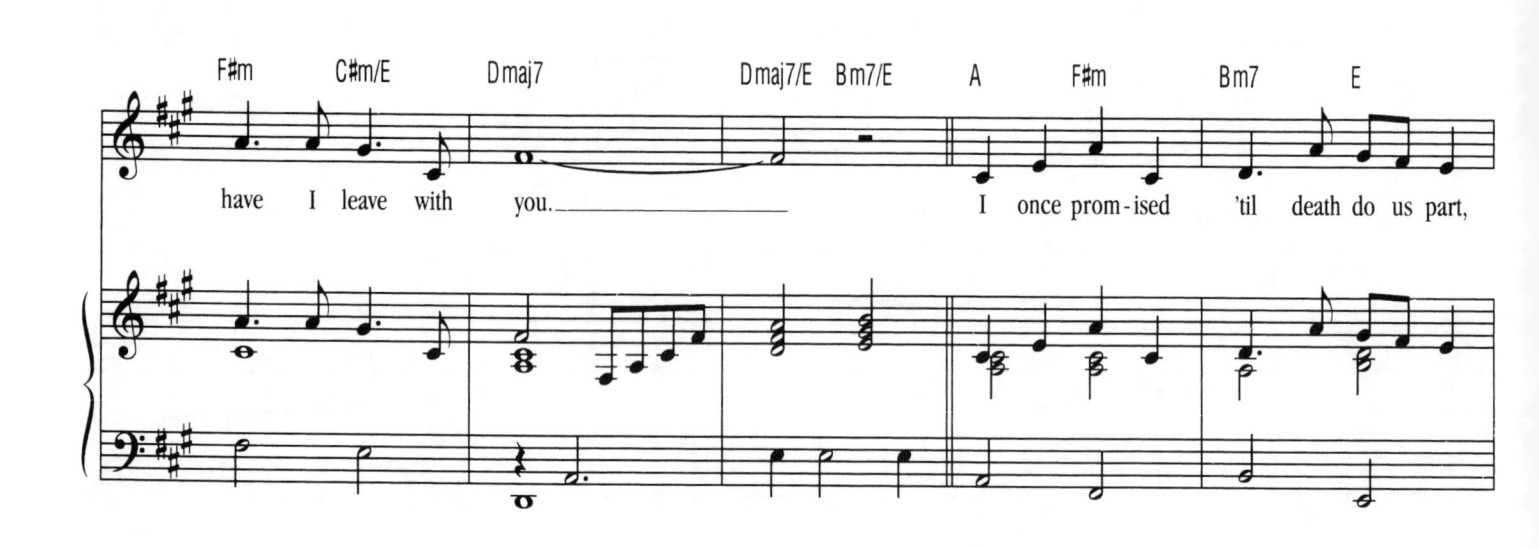

Moderato

John
You know that our part-ing breaks my heart. I have nev-er felt such sor-row. All the love I have I leave with you. _____ I once prom-ised 'til death do us part, and yet I'll be gone to-mor-row. Please be-lieve me what I said was true. But

© Copyright 2000 Andrew Lloyd Webber licensed to The Really Useful Group Ltd.
International Copyright Secured   All Rights Reserved

when I go, I'm on my own. The path I walk I walk a-lone. I face a bit-ter world with on-ly mem-'ries to guide me. I care more than I have ev-er cared, yet I know that I am leav-ing. You'll be in my heart the whole life through. And all the love I have, I leave with

24

Mary: You're a father, you've a family. Your son needs you, don't ignore him, you. just to fight a war you cannot win.

John: I hope my son will be proud of me. When I fight, I'm fighting for him. Share the love I leave for you with him.

Mary: And so we all must pay the price for

such a stu-pid sa-cri-fice. Don't you un-der-stand that this won't end 'til we let it.

John
When I'm gone you know I won't be back. Mine's a path that has no turn-ing. Please be-lieve me what I said was true, that all the love I have I leave with you.

Don't Like You
from *The Beautiful Game*

Music by Andrew Lloyd Webber
Lyrics by Ben Elton

Moderato

Mary: Don't like you. Don't like you. I _____ don't think I like you. You're bad, you're sad, and

© Copyright 2000 Andrew Lloyd Webber licensed to The Really Useful Group Ltd.
International Copyright Secured   All Rights Reserved

I_____ know ni-cer boys. Not both-ered. **John:** Not both-ered. I sim-ply am not both-ered. You're vain a to-tal pain and I_____ know sweet-er girls. You've been hang-ing round my door and watch-ing me at school. **Mary:** Yes and I was think-ing you're com-plete-ly un-cool. **John:** Well I

Bb7
F
Mary
John
would - n't say your - self was much to shout a - bout. Do your fly up son - ny 'cos your brain's hang - ing out. You're
C
C+
Dm
Mary
Both
gag - ging for a date, I know you're dy - ing to meet. I don't think so while there's still a dog left out on the street. That's
Bb7
F
fine by me, I don't like you.
F
F
Bb
Mary
Don't need you. Don't want you. I can live with-

out you. I swear I just don't care be-cause I____ know nic-er boys.

John
Don't like you. Don't need you. I____ don't care a-bout you. You see, you're not for me. I like lots____ of oth-er

girls.

Mary: You bug me and you're ugly and your jokes are a bore, your efforts at coherent conversation are poor. The lights are clearly on but then there's nobody home.

John: In that case why the hell d'you call me up on the phone?

Mary: I never flipping did, sure it was you who called me.

John: Well what the hell, at least there's one thing that we agree.

Both: I'm damned sure I don't

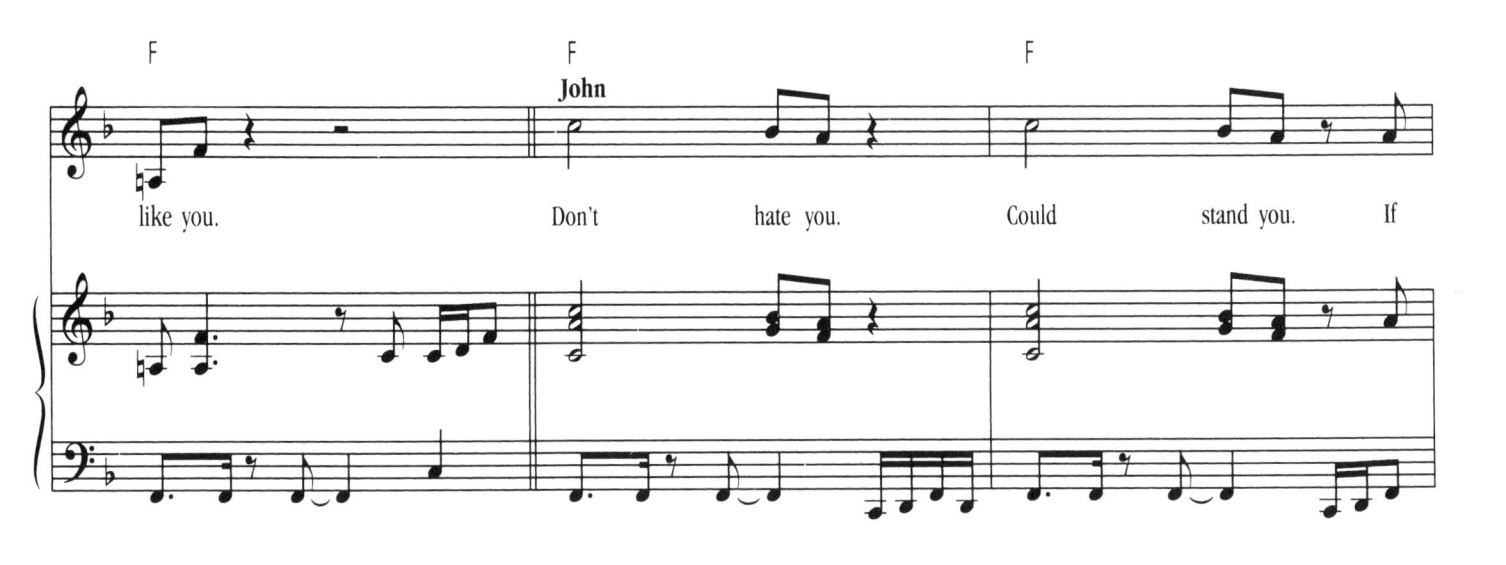

like you. Don't hate you. Could stand you. If pushed could tolerate you. I'm sure that you'll mat- ure, I have known more stupid boys.

Mary: You say it. **John:** No you say it. **Mary:** Alright— I vaguely like you. It's bad, I must be mad. But I think— we could be friends. **John:** No commitment, only

F F F
Mary
John
friends. I like you. I like you.
B♭ F C
Both
Yes, I think I like you. It's real, It's how I
Dm B♭ F
feel and I want to be your girl / boy

The First Time
from *The Beautiful Game*

Music by Andrew Lloyd Webber
Lyrics by Ben Elton

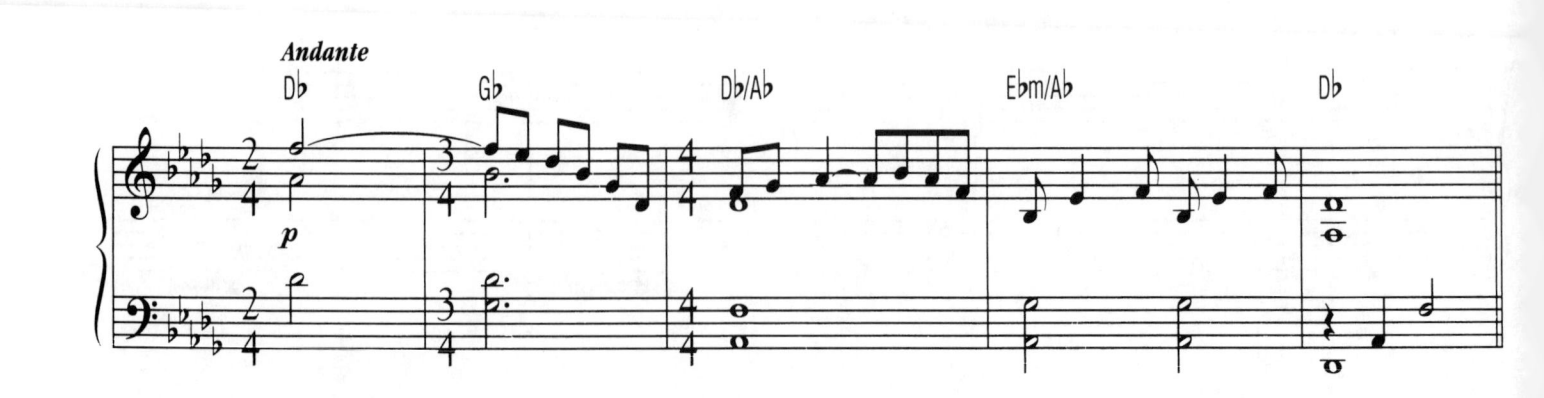

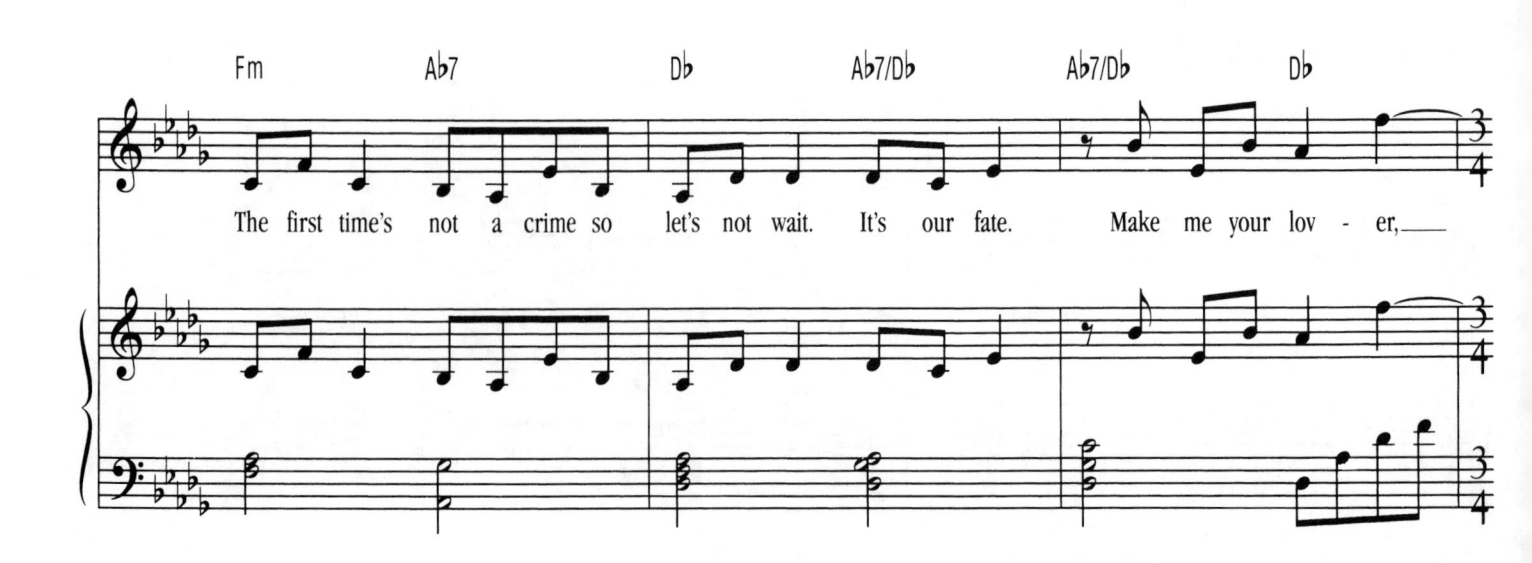

Andante

Mary: Can this be? You and me? Scared of each oth-er. Why do I trem-ble? The first time's not a crime so let's not wait. It's our fate. Make me your lov-er,

© Copyright 2000 Andrew Lloyd Webber licensed to The Really Useful Group Ltd.
International Copyright Secured   All Rights Reserved

— this moment must be so sublime, a night of pure bliss, for us this first time. From now on the only girl you'll need is me. I am yours until my dying day. From this night when we share our virginity We'll be together come what may.

What if I'm not sub-lime? No Ca-sa-no-va. I've had a cou-ple. Birth-day suit. Brew-er's droop. I'm so shy. How can I get my leg o-ver? Hope there's lead in my pen-cil when I lose my cher-ry this ver-y first time. Have I got all the right in-form-a-tion. Which posi - tion does a girl pre - fer? I fear pre - ma - ture e - jac - u - la - tion. 'Cos my God I don't half fan - cy her.

Mary: If I seem less than keen, it's not e - va - sion. I'm scared I'll be a piece of wood, not much good.

John: Close my eyes, try to rise to the oc - ca - sion.

Gmaj7
Both
Db/Ab
Ebm/Ab
Let's face it we're just pet - ri - fied. So let's get to this and through this first
Db
Bbm
Gbmaj7
Db
time. It's ab - surd, this mom - ent's all we've dreamt a - bout. When our
Bbm
Gbmaj7
Bbm
Bbm
Gbmaj7
love will set our spir - its free. I don't care if I don't make you
Db
Gb
Gbm
Db
scream and shout. I love you and know that you love me.

Mary: Why do I want to cry_____ when I'm so hap-py?

John: I don't de-serve this. Look at you, a dream come true. I'm on my knees, hold me please_____ Now and for-ev-er._____

Both: I'll keep you close and make you mine,___ right from the first kiss, for us, this first time. No one ev-er felt the way I feel to-night. No de-sire ev-er felt so strong. Sparks of pas-sion glow-ing hot and shin-ing bright. A fire to burn my whole life long.

Mary
You and me, young and free, in love for-ev-er.

John
I am your hus-band.

F♯m A7 D A7/D
Mary
Both
I'm your wife. In love for life. So hold me tight. Through the night,
f
A7/D D Gmaj7 D/A
we'll be to-geth - er. We'll move the Heav - ens and the Earth. We'll make a
Em/A D Gmaj7
new star, for this, our first time.
D/A Em/A D
Colla Voce
We'll make a new star, for this, our first time.

To Have and to Hold

from *The Beautiful Game*

Music by Andrew Lloyd Webber
Lyrics by Ben Elton

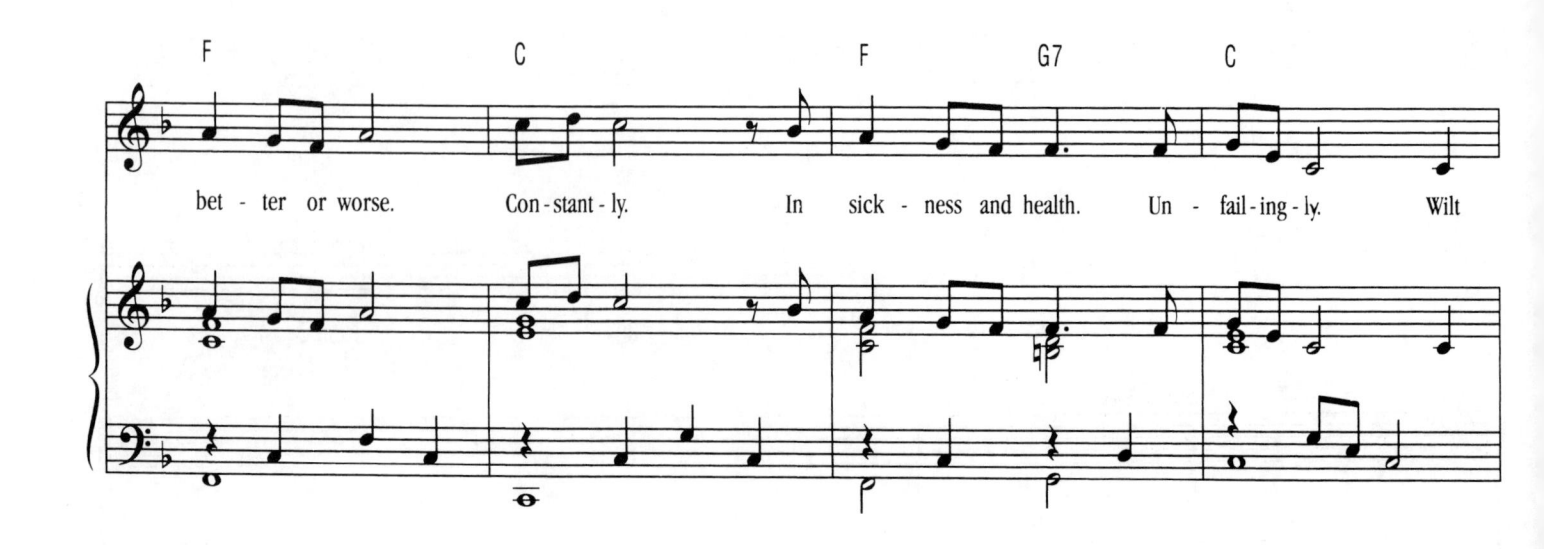

John: To have and to hold. Faith-ful-ly. To hon-our and love. De-vot-ed-ly. Wilt thou take this man? **Mary:** Yes I will. For better or worse. Con-stant-ly. In sick-ness and health. Un-fail-ing-ly. Wilt

© Copyright 2000 Andrew Lloyd Webber licensed to The Really Useful Group Ltd.
International Copyright Secured All Rights Reserved

| Bb | A7 | Dm | Bb | Csus4 | C |

John
thou take this girl? Yes I will.

| Bb | C7 | F | Dm |

Both
I pledge my soul to you I give you my heart.

| Bb | Gm/Bb | Gm7 | C |

Chorus
There by your side un-til death do us part. To

| F | C | F | G7 | C |

hon-our and love. Con-stant-ly 'Til death do them part. De-vot-ed-ly. Yes from this wedding day forth joined by God. To be by your side. Faithfully. Forsaking all others. Willingly. With my body I thee worship, and with this ring I thee wed. To have and to hold.

Fer-vent-ly. To hon-our and love. Un-end-ing-ly. Wilt thou take this man / girl? Yes I will. And wilt thou take this man for bet-ter and for worse? And wilt thou take this girl in sick-ness and in health? And wilt thou take this heart?

Gus: The Theatre Cat
from *Cats*

Music by Andrew Lloyd Webber
Text by T.S. Eliot

♩ = 108

SOLO:

Gus is the / Cat at the Thea-tre Door. His name as I ought to have told you be-fore, is real-ly As-par-a-gus. But that's such a

coat's ver-y / shab-by, he's thin as a rake, And he suf-fers from pal-sy that makes his paw shake. Yet he was, in his youth, quite the smart-est of

played, in my / time, ev-'ry pos-si-ble part And I used to know sev-en-ty speech-es by heart. I'd ex-tem-po-rize back-chat, I knew how to

knew how to / act with my back and my tail; With an hour of re-hears-al, I nev-er could fail. I'd a voice that would soft-en the hard-est of

---

Music Copyright © 1981 Andrew Lloyd Webber licensed to The Really Useful Group Ltd.
Text Copyright © 1939 T.S. Eliot; this edition of the text © 1981 Set Copyrights Ltd.
All Rights in the text Controlled by Faber and Faber Ltd. and Administered for the United States and Canada by R&H Music Co.
International Copyright Secured   All Rights Reserved

(sheet music)

palm - i - est days. For he once was a Star of the high - est de - gree: He has
likes to re - late his suc - cess on the Halls, Where the

act - ed with Irv - ing, he's act - ed with Tree. And he
Gal - ler - y once gave him sev - en cat - calls. But his

grand - est cre - a - tion, as he loves to tell, Was Fire - frore - fid - dle, the

Fiend of the Fell.

D.S. al Coda
GUS: I have

CODA

cat. But my grand-est cre-a-tion, as his-t'ry will tell, Was Fire-frore-fid-dle, the Fiend of the Fell.

Più mosso

SOLO: Then, if some-one will give him a tooth-ful of gin, He will tell how he once played a part in "East Lynne". At a Shake-speare per-for-mance he once walked on pat, When some act-or sug-gest-ed the need for a cat. And I

Meno mosso

say: Now, these kit-tens, they do not get trained As we did in the days when Vic-
nev-er get drilled in a reg-u-lar troupe, And they think they are smart, just to

tor-i-a reigned. They
jump through a hoop. And he says as he scratch-es him-self with his

GUS: claws: Well, the Thea-tre is cer-tain-ly not what it was. These mod-ern productions are all ver-y well, But there's noth-ing to e-qual, from what I hear

tell, That mo-ment of mys-ter-y When I made his-to-ry As

Fire - frore - fid-dle, the Fiend of the Fell.

And I once crossed the stage on a tel-e-graph wire, To

rescue a child when a house was on fire. And I think that I still can much better than most, Produced blood-curdling noises to bring on the Ghost. I once played Growltiger, could do it again, could do it again, could do it again.

Memory
from *Cats*

Music by Andrew Lloyd Webber
Text by Trevor Nunn after T.S. Eliot

Flowing

Baritone or Tenor: Mid - night. Not a sound from the pave - ment. Has the moon lost her mem - 'ry? She is smil-ing a - lone. In the lamp - light the with-ered leaves col -

Music Copyright © 1981 Andrew Lloyd Webber licensed to The Really Useful Group Ltd.
Text Copyright © 1981 Trevor Nunn and Set Copyrights Ltd.
All Rights in the text Controlled by Faber and Faber Ltd. and Administered for the United States and Canada by R&H Music Co.
International Copyright Secured   All Rights Reserved

lect at my feet ___ And the wind ___ be-gins to moan.

Mem-'ry. ___ All a-lone in the moon-light ___ I can smile at the old days, ___ I was beau-ti-ful then. ___ I re-mem-ber the time I knew what hap-pi-ness was, ___ Let the

mem-'ry live a-gain. Ev'-ry street lamp

mem-'ry live a-gain. Ev'-ry street lamp

seems to beat___ a fa-tal-is-tic warn-ing.

seems to beat___ a fa-tal-is-tic warn-ing.

Some-one mut-ters___ and a street lamp gut-ters___ and soon it will be

Some-one mut-ters___ and a street lamp gut-ters___ and soon it will be morn-ing. Day-light. I must wait for the sun-rise, I must think of a new life And I must-n't give in. When the dawn comes to-night will be a mem-o-ry too And a new day will be-gin.

Burnt out ends of smoky days, _____ the stale cold smell _____ of morn-ing. The street lamp dies an-oth-er

cresc.
night is o - ver an - oth - er day is dawn - ing.
cresc.
an - oth - er day is dawn - ing.
cresc.
Touch me. Eas - y to leave me with the
Touch me. It's so eas - y to leave me All a - lone with the
8va
poco rit.
a tempo
mp
mem - o - ry Of my days in the sun. If you
mem - 'ry Of my days in the sun. If you
loco

touch me you'll un-der-stand what hap-pi-ness is. Look, a

touch me you'll un-der-stand what hap-pi-ness is. Look, a

new day has be-gun.

new day has be-gun.

All I Ask of You

from *The Phantom of the Opera*

Music by Andrew Lloyd Webber
Lyrics by Charles Hart
Additional Lyrics by Richard Stilgoe

Andante

RAOUL: No more talk of darkness, forget these wide-eyed fears: I'm here, nothing can harm you, my words will warm and calm you. Let me be your freedom, let daylight dry your tears: I'm

© Copyright 1986 Andrew Lloyd Webber licensed to The Really Useful Group Ltd.
International Copyright Secured All Rights Reserved

touch me you'll un-der-stand what hap-pi-ness is. Look, a

touch me you'll un-der-stand what hap-pi-ness is. Look, a

new day has be-gun.

new day has be-gun.

All I Ask of You
from *The Phantom of the Opera*

Music by Andrew Lloyd Webber
Lyrics by Charles Hart
Additional Lyrics by Richard Stilgoe

Andante

RAOUL:
No more talk of dark-ness, for - get these wide-eyed fears: I'm here, noth-ing can harm you, my words will warm and calm you. Let me be your free-dom, let day-light dry your tears: I'm

© Copyright 1986 Andrew Lloyd Webber licensed to The Really Useful Group Ltd.
International Copyright Secured   All Rights Reserved

here, with you, be - side you, to guard you and to guide you.

CHRISTINE: Say you love me ev - ery wak - ing mo - ment, turn my head with talk of sum - mer - time. Say you need me with you now and al - ways; prom - ise me that all you say is true, that's all I ask of

RAOUL: Let me be your shelter, let me be your light; you're safe, no one will find you your fears are far behind you.

CHRISTINE: All I want is freedom, a world with no more night; and you, always beside me, to hold me and to hide me.

RAOUL: Then say you'll share with me one love, one lifetime; let me lead you from your solitude.

Db Bbm7 Ebm7 Ab Db/F Gb
Say you need me with you, here be - side you, an - y - where you go, let me go
Db/Ab Ebm7/Ab Ab6 Ebm7/Ab Db Bbm7
CHRISTINE:
too. Chris - tine, that's all I ask of you.
Say you'll share with me one
rit.
molto rit.
a tempo
f
Ebm7 Ab Db/F Bbm7 Ebm7 Ab Ab7
love, one life - time; say the word and I will fol - low you.
Db Bbm7 Ebm7 Ab Db/F Gb
TOGETHER:
Share each day with me, each night, each morn - ing.
CHRISTINE:
Say you love me!
RAOUL:
You know I
rit.

Db/Ab Ebm7/Ab Ab6 Ebm7/Ab Db Bbm7
RAOUL & CHRISTINE:
do. Love me, that's all I ask of you.
molto rit.
a tempo
Ebm7 Ab Db/F Bbm7 Ebm7 G/Ab Ab Ab6 Ab9
Db Bbm7 Ebm7 Ab Db/F Gb
CHRISTINE & RAOUL:
An - y - where you go, let me go
f
ff largo
Db/Ab Ebm7/Ab Ab6 Ebm7/Ab Db
RAOUL & CHRISTINE:
too; love me, that's all I ask of you.
mp
molto rit.

The Point of No Return
from *The Phantom of the Opera*

Music by Andrew Lloyd Webber
Lyrics by Charles Hart
Additional Lyrics by Richard Stilgoe

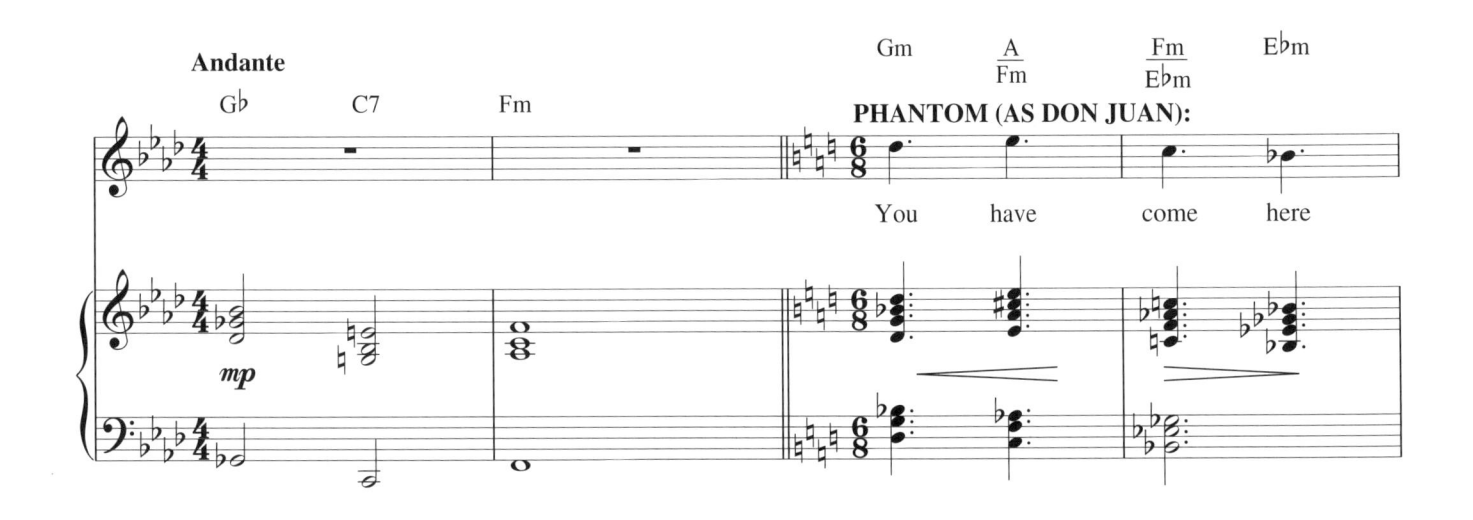

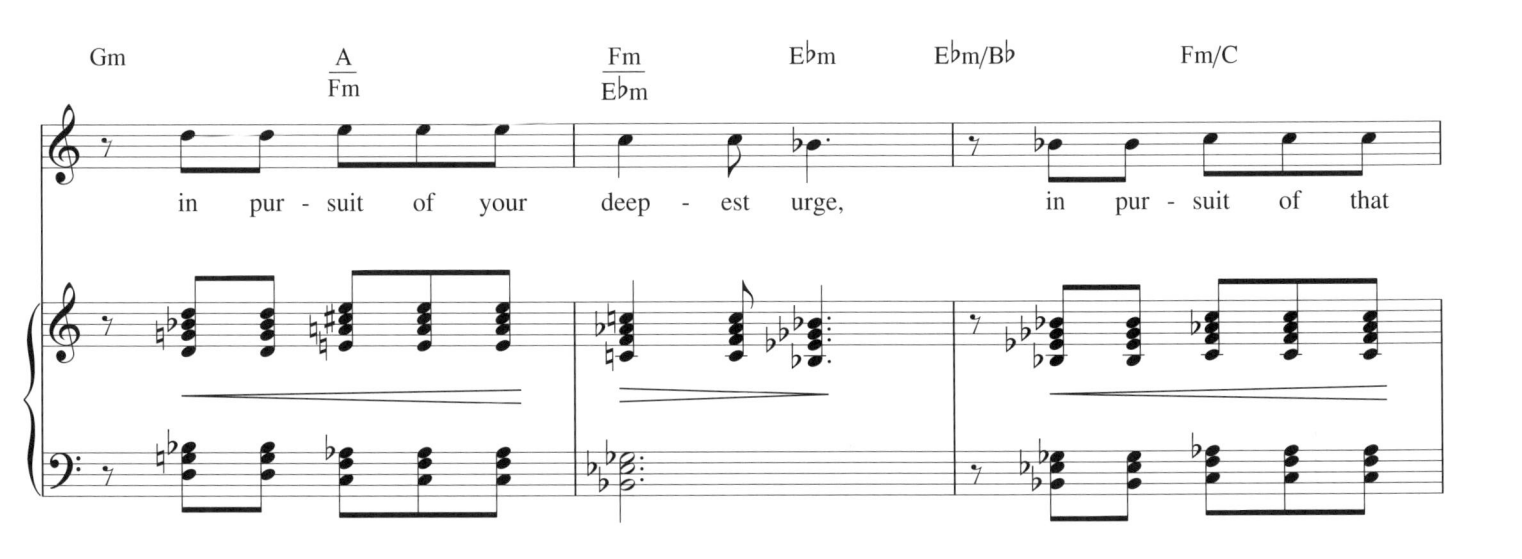

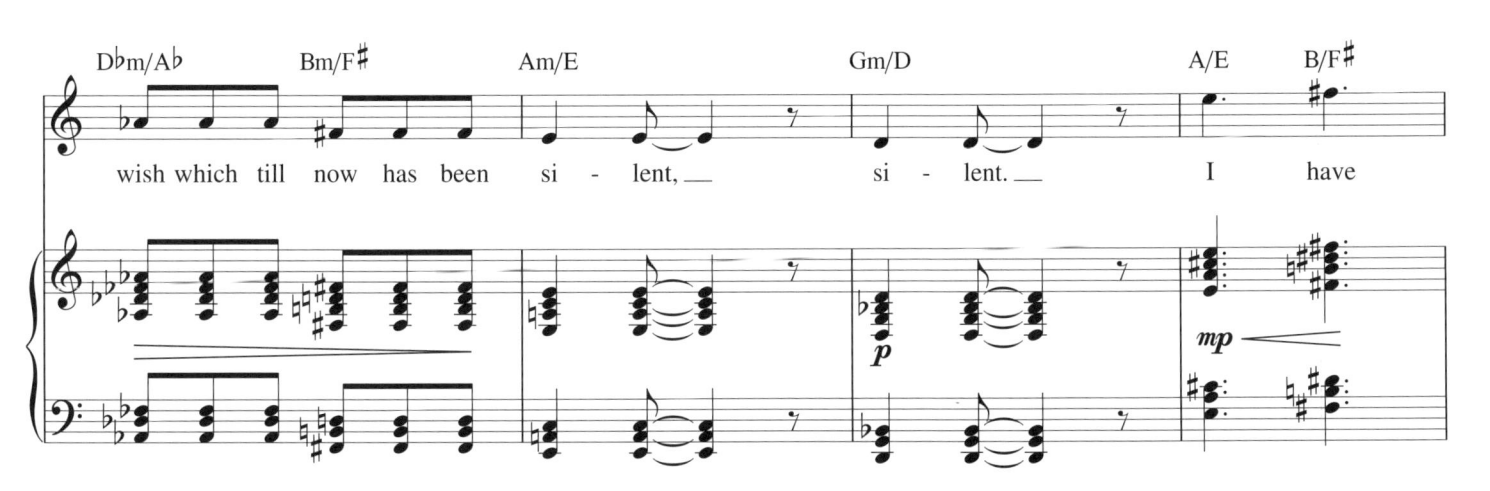

Andante

PHANTOM (AS DON JUAN):
You have come here in pur-suit of your deep-est urge, in pur-suit of that wish which till now has been si - lent, si - lent. I have

© Copyright 1986 Andrew Lloyd Webber licensed to The Really Useful Group Ltd.
International Copyright Secured   All Rights Reserved

brought you that our pas-sions may fuse and merge.

In your mind you've al-read-y suc-cumbed to me, dropped all de-fenc-es, com-

plete-ly suc-cumbed to me, now you are here with me, no sec-ond thoughts, you've de-

cid-ed,____ de-cid-ed.____

Allegretto

Past the point of no return, no backward glances; the games of make believe are at an end. Past all thought of "if" or "when," no use resisting, a-

-bandon thought and let the dream de-scend. What rag-ing fire shall flood the soul? What rich de-sire un-locks its door? What sweet se-duc-tion lies be-fore us? Past the point of no re - turn, the fi - nal thresh - old, what warm un - spo - ken se - crets will we learn be - yond the point of no re - turn?

Tempo I

CHRISTINE (AS AMINTA):
You have brought me to that mo - ment where words run dry,

to that mo - ment where speech dis - ap - pears in - to si - lence, si - lence. I have come here hard - ly know - ing the rea - son why, in my mind I've al - read - y i - mag - ined our bod - ies en - twin - ing, de -

fence-less and si-lent and now I am here with you, no sec-ond thoughts, I've de-cid-ed, _____ de - cid - ed. _____

Past _____ the point of no re-turn, no go-ing back now, our pas-sion play has now at last be-gun.

Past all thought of right or wrong, one final question; how long should we two wait be-fore we're one? When will the blood be-gin to race? The sleep-ing bud burst in-to

73

bloom? When will the flames at last con-sume us?

TOGETHER:
Past the point of no return, the final threshold, the bridge is crossed, so stand and watch it burn. We've passed the point of no return.

The Phantom of the Opera
from *The Phantom of the Opera*

Music by Andrew Lloyd Webber
Lyrics by Charles Hart
Additional Lyrics by Richard Stilgoe and Mike Batt

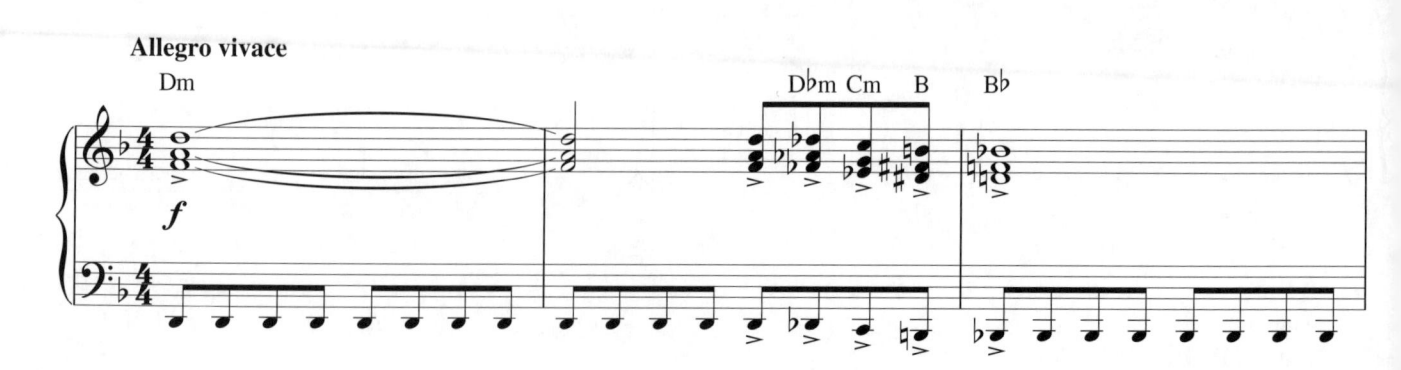

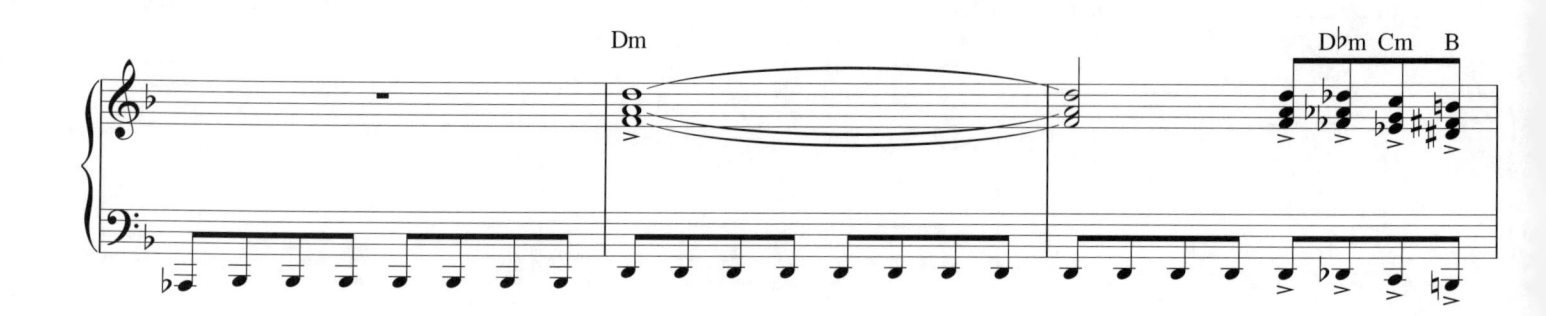

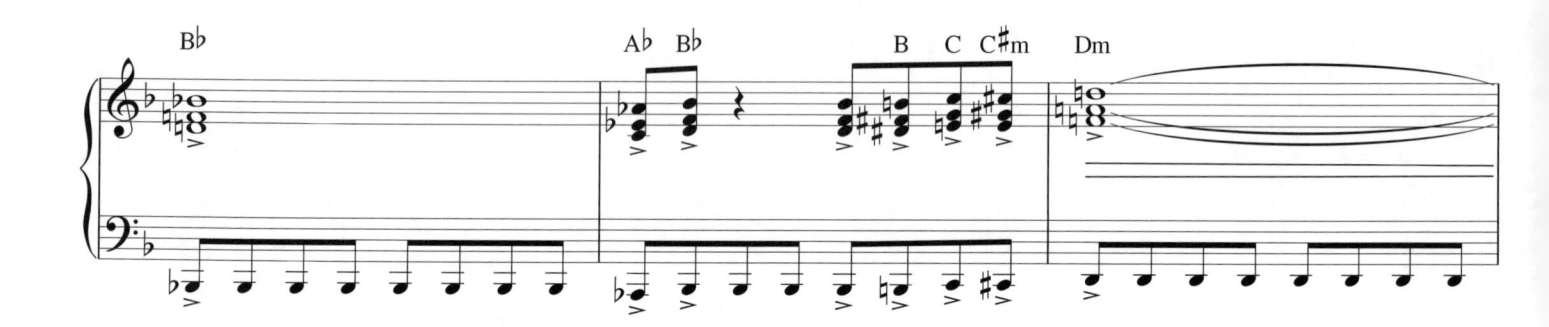

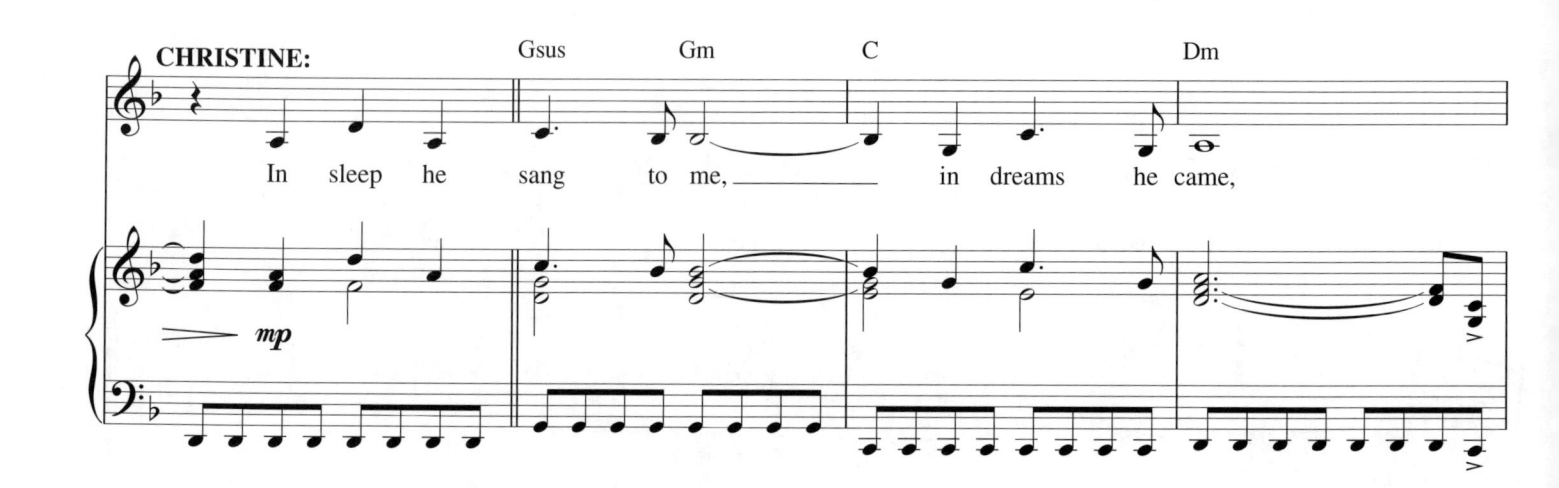

Christine: In sleep he sang to me, in dreams he came,

© Copyright 1986 Andrew Lloyd Webber licensed to The Really Useful Group Ltd.
International Copyright Secured   All Rights Reserved

that voice which calls to me and speaks my name.

And do I dream again? for now I find the phan- tom of the op-er-a is there in-side my mind.

B♭
A♭ B♭
D♭dim
Gm
PHANTOM:
Sing once a -
mf
Csus
Cm
F
Gm
gain with me our strange du - et; my pow - er
Csus
Cm
F
Gm
o - ver you grows strong - er yet. And though you
E♭maj7
Cm/E♭
F
Gm
turn from me to glance be - hind, the

phan - tom of the op-er-a is there _____ in - side your mind. _____

CHRISTINE: Those who have seen your face _____ draw back in fear. _____ I am the mask you wear, _____ it's me they

Em/B
PHANTOM & CHRISTINE:
Cmaj7
Am/C
D
hear. {Your / My} spi - rit and {my / your} voice in one com-
Em
bined; the phan - tom of the op-er-a is
Cdim
VOICES:
Em
there in - side {my / your} mind.
He's there, the phan - tom of the
C
Em
op - era. Be - ware the phan - tom of the

op - era.

PHANTOM: In all your fan - ta - sies, you always knew that man and mys - ter - y were both in you.

PHANTOM & CHRISTINE: And in this lab - y - rinth where night is blind, the

Fm
D♭dim
phan - tom of the op - er - a is there in - side my your
Fm
PHANTOM:
D♭
CHRISTINE:
mind.
(Spoken:) Sing, my angel of music!
He's
Fm
D♭
there the phan - tom of the op - era.
Fm
D♭
Ah!
PHANTOM: Sing, my angel, sing!

Gm
CHRISTINE:
E♭
1
Ah!
PHANTOM: (1st time only) Sing for me!
3
2
Am
CHRISTINE:
F
Ah!
PHANTOM: Sing, my
angel of music!
Am
CHRISTINE:
F
Ah!
Ah!
Am
Ah!
Ah!

Pie Jesu
from *Requiem*

By Andrew Lloyd Webber

Je - su, qui tol - lis pec - ca - ta mun - di, do - na e - is re - qui - em, do - na e - is re - qui - em.

Pi - e Je - su, pi - e Je - su, pi - e Je - su, pi - e Je - su, qui tol - lis pec-ca-ta mun-di, do - na e - is re-qui-em,___ do - na e - is re-qui-em.___ Ag-nus De - i,___ Ag-nus De - i,___ Ag-nus De - i,___ Ag-nus

85

Dei, qui tollis peccata mundi, dona eis requiem, dona eis requiem sempiternam, sempiternam, requiem.

Dei, qui tollis peccata mundi, dona eis requiem, dona eis requiem sempiternam, sempiternam, sempiternam.

Only You
from *Starlight Express*

Music by Andrew Lloyd Webber
Words by Richard Stilgoe

Moderately slow

SHE: On-ly you have the pow-er to move me. And to-geth-er we make the whole world move in sym-pa-thy, but I could not see be-fore. ***HE:** On-ly

*Male part is to be sung up an octave throughout.

© Copyright 1984 Andrew Lloyd Webber licensed to The Really Useful Group Ltd.
International Copyright Secured   All Rights Reserved

you ___ have the pow-er to move me, ___ take me, hold me, mold me, change me and im-prove me. ___ It's not fun-ny ___ an-y-more. ___

SHE: There was I ___ won-d'ring why
HE: There was I, ___ I was won-d'ring why ___
BOTH: ev-'ry day dis-ap-peared ___ in-to the dis - tance. Now with

you the light is shin-ing through. **SHE:** You gave me life not just ex-

-ist-ence. **HE:** On - ly you **SHE:** You are the star-

-light. have the pow-er to move me. We can a-chieve.

And to-geth-er we make the whole world move in sym-pa-thy. On - ly
The whole world move in sym-pa-thy.

you have the pow - er__ to move__ me.__

SHE: There was I_____ won d'ring why_____ ev -'ry day__
HE: There was I,_____ I was won-d'ring why__ ev -'ry day__

dis-ap-peared into the dis-tance. Now with you the light is shin-ing through. You gave me life not just ex-ist-ence.

SHE: On - ly you, only you have the pow-er to move me.
HE: On - ly you, only you have the pow-er to move me.

And to-geth-er we'll make the whole world move in sym-pa-thy,

F♯m7 A/B E G♯m7
SHE:
but I could not see be - fore.
HE: No, I could - n't see be -
A A/B E G♯m7 A A/B
And on - ly you have the pow - er to
fore. And
E G♯m7 A A/B G♯m C♯m
SHE:
move me, take me, hold me, mold me, change me and im - prove - me. On - ly
F♯m7 A/B A6 E
BOTH:
you have the pow - er to move me.

Too Much in Love to Care
from *Sunset Boulevard*

Music by Andrew Lloyd Webber
Lyrics by Don Black and Christopher Hampton

BETTY: When I was a kid I played in this street, I always loved illusion. I thought make believe was truer than life, but

© Copyright 1993 Andrew Lloyd Webber licensed to The Really Useful Group Ltd.
International Copyright Secured   All Rights Reserved

now it's all con-fu-sion. Please can you tell me what's happen-ing? I just don't know an-y-more. If this is real, how should I feel? What should I look for? *rit.* **JOE:** *a tempo* If you were smart, you would keep on walk-ing out of my life, as fast as you can.

I'm not the one you should pin your hopes on, you're fall-ing for the wrong kind of man. This is cra-zy. You know we should call it a day. Sound ad-vice, great ad-vice, let's throw it a-way. I can't con-trol all the things I'm feel-ing, I have-n't got a prayer.

If I'm a fool, well, I'm too much in love to care. I know where I was, I'd given up hope, made friends with dis-il-lu-sion. No one in my life, but I look at you, and now it's all con-fu-sion.

BETTY: Please can you tell me what's

Bm7 Em A7 Bm
happen - ing? I just don't know an - y - more. If this is real,
Bm/G♯ Em7 A7
how should I feel? What should I look for?
Meno mosso
D Bm7
I thought I had
Em A7 D Bm7 Em7 A7
ev - 'ry-thing I need - ed. My life was set, my dreams were in place.
D Bm7 Em A D Bm
My heart could see way in - to the fu - ture. All of that goes when

Em7 A D/F♯ F♯m7 D F♯m7
I see your face. I should hate you, there I was, the world in my hand.
G Em7 A7 D Bm7
rall. a tempo
Can one kiss kiss a-way ev-'ry-thing I planned? I can't con-trol
Em7 A7 D D7 G
all the things I'm feel-ing. I'm float-ing in mid - air.
C Gmaj7/F♯ Asus A7 D
rall. a tempo
I know it's wrong, but I'm too much in love to care.

Poco meno mosso
F/C Dm7 Gm/C C7 F Dm
BOTH:
I thought I had ev - 'ry-thing I need - ed. My life was set, my
Gm7 C F Dm7 Gm7 C7
dreams were in place. My heart could see way in - to the fu - ture.
F Dm7 Gm7 C7 F Am
All of that goes when I see your face. This is cra - zy.
F Am B♭ Gm7 C
JOE:
BETTY:
BOTH:
You know we should call it a day. Sound ad-vice, great ad-vice, let's throw it a - way.
3
3

I can't control all the things I'm feeling. We're floating in mid-air. If we are fools, well, we're too much in love to care. If we are fools, well, we're too much in love too care.

Amigos Para Siempre
(Friends for Life)
(The Official Theme of the Barcelona 1992 Games)

Music by Andrew Lloyd Webber
Lyrics by Don Black

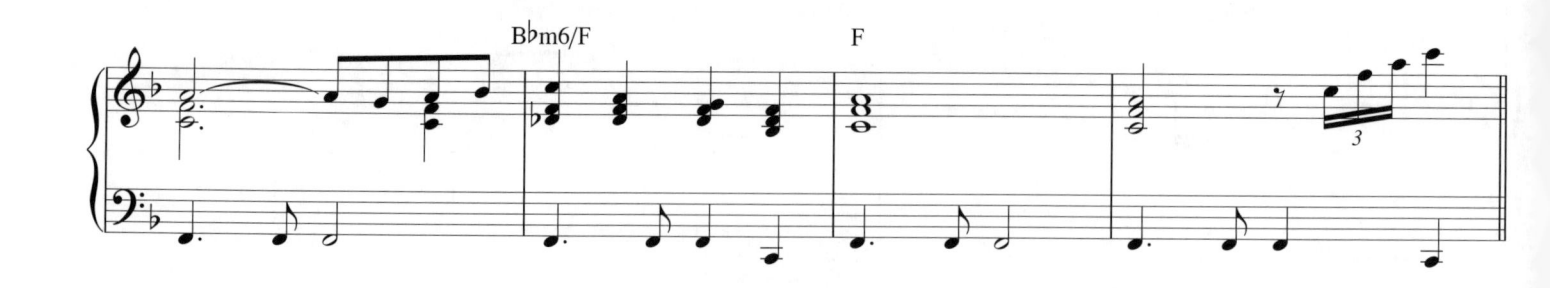

Gentle habañera feel

SHE:
I _____ don't have to say a word to you, _____ you seem to know what - ev - er mood I'm go - ing through. Feel as though I've known you for - ev - er.
We _____ share mem - o - ries I won't for - get. _____ And we'll share more, my friend, we haven't start - ed yet. Some - thing hap - pens when we're to - geth - er.

© Copyright 1992 Andrew Lloyd Webber licensed to The Really Useful Group Ltd.
International Copyright Secured   All Rights Reserved

HE:

You can look in-to my eyes and see the way I feel and how the world is treat-ing me. May-be I have known you for-ev-er.

When I look at you I won-der why there has to come a time when we must say good-bye. I'm a-live when we are to-geth-er.

BOTH:* "A-mi-gos pa-ra siem-pre" means you'll al-ways be my friend. "A-mi-gos pa-ra siem-pre" means a love that can-not end. Friends for life, not just a sum-mer or a

The top notes are to be sung by the male voice, the bottom by the female voice.

spring, a - mi - gos pa - ra siem - pre. I feel you near me e - ven when we are a -

part. Just know-ing you are in this world can warm my heart. Friends for

life, not just a sum-mer or a spring, a - mi - gos pa - ra siem - pre.

Maestoso

B♭m
D♭m
A♭
HE:
A♭maj7
When I look at you I won - der why there has to
B♭m/A♭
BOTH:
D♭m/A♭
A♭
come a time when we must say good - bye I'm a - live when we are to - geth - er.
D♭
E♭9
"A - mi - gos pa - ra siem - pre" means you'll al - ways be my friend. "A - mi - gos pa - ra
rall.
a tempo

A♭
Fm7
B♭m7
siem-pre" means a love that can-not end. Friends for life not just a sum-mer or a
E♭7
D♭
A♭
spring, a-mi-gos pa-ra siem - pre. I feel you
D♭
E♭9
A♭
near me e-ven when we are a - part. Just know-ing you are in this world can warm my
Fm7
B♭m
E♭7
heart. Friends for life, not just a sum-mer or a spring, a-mi-gos pa-ra

siem - pre._____ "A - mi - gos pa - ra siem - pre" means you'll al - ways be my friend. "A - mi - gos pa - ra siem - pre" means a love that can - not end. Friends for life, not just a sum - mer or a spring, a - mi - gos pa - ra siem - pre, a - mi - gos pa - ra siem - pre._____

* The top notes are to be sung by the female voice, the bottom by the male voice.

I Believe My Heart
from *The Woman in White*

Music by Andrew Lloyd Webber
Lyrics by David Zippel

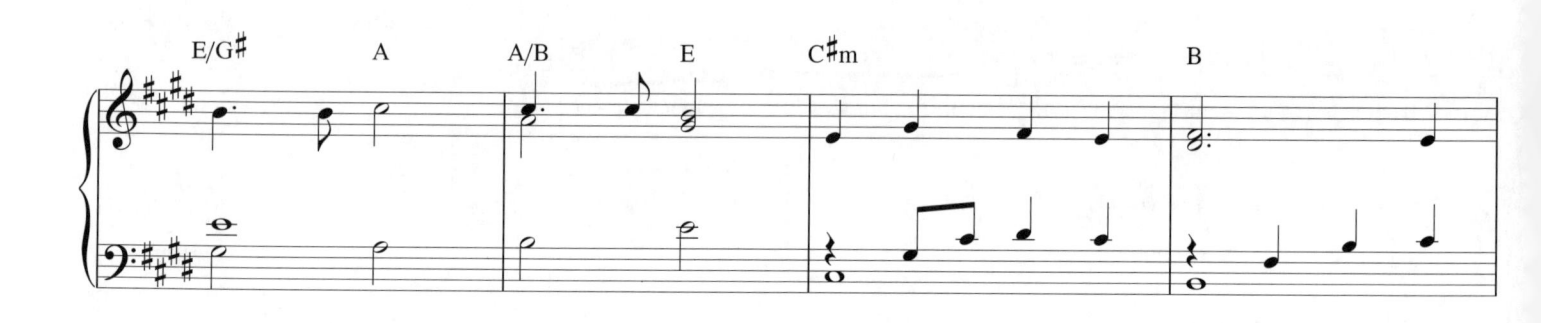

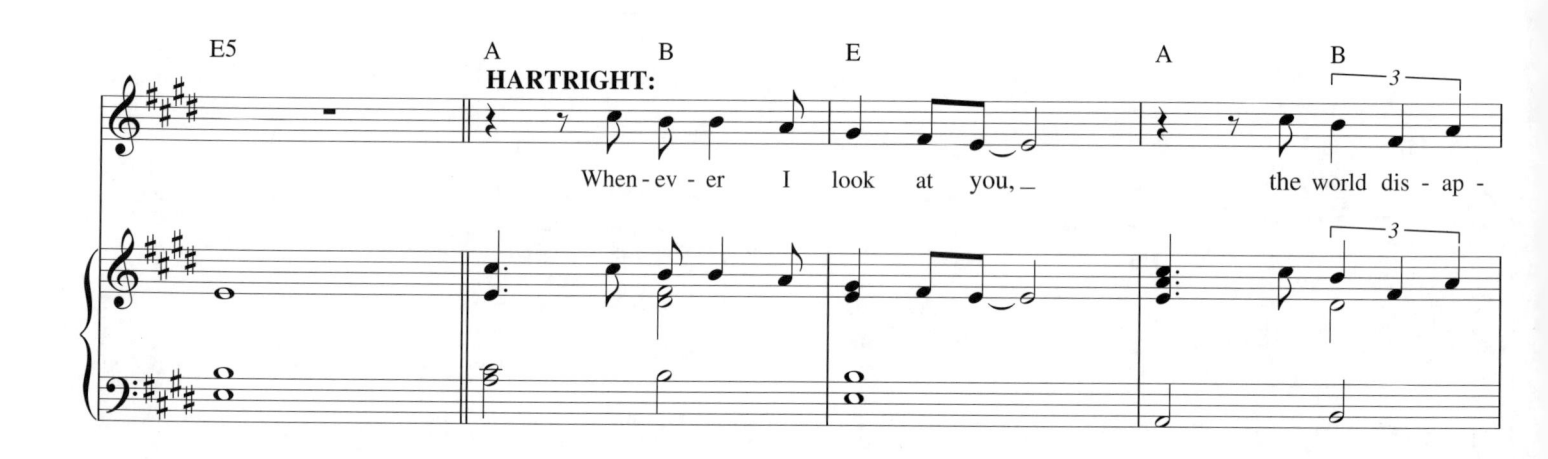

HARTRIGHT: When-ev-er I look at you,__ the world dis-ap-pears. All in a sin-gle glance so re-veal-ing.__

Music © Copyright 2004, 2005 by Andrew Lloyd Webber licensed to The Really Useful Group Ltd.
Lyric © Copyright 2004, 2005 by In Your Ear Music
In Your Ear Music Administered throughout the World excluding the UK and Eire by Williamson Music
International Copyright Secured   All Rights Reserved

A B E
You smile and I feel as though
A B E A
I've known you for years. How do I know to
E/G♯ F♯ B
trust what I'm feel - ing?
E B7/E E A E
LAURA:
I be - lieve my heart. What else can I

108

do when ev-'ry part of ev-'ry thought leads me straight to you?

HARTRIGHT: I believe my heart.

There's no oth-er choice, for now when-ev-er my heart speaks I can on-ly hear your voice.

LAURA: The life-time be-fore we met has fad-ed a-way.

HARTRIGHT: How did I live a mo-ment with-out you?

LAURA: You don't have to speak at all, I know what you'd say.

HARTRIGHT: And I know ev-'ry se-cret a-bout you. I be-lieve my heart. It be-lieves in you. It's tell-ing me that what I see is com-plete-ly true.

LAURA: I be-lieve my heart. How can it be

wrong? It says that what I feel for you, I will feel my whole life long.

BOTH: I believe my heart. It believes in you. It's telling me that what I see

F♯m
Bm7/E
E7
A
E7/A
is com - plete - ly true.
And with all my
A
D
A
E
soul
I be - lieve my heart.
The
A/C♯
D
E9
A
F♯m
por - trait that it paints of you
is a per - fect
Bm7/E
E7
A
Bm7/A
A
work of art.
ff